The Bullying From The Beginning

Introduction-Chapter 1

I want to get a couple of things out in the open right off the bat. This book is not a boo-hoo, look at me, I was bullied in school, please feel sorry for me type of thing. Was the amount and severity of bullying that I received any worse than what others have seen? Probably not. There has been a lot of attention brought to light when kids that were bullied in school either take their own life or lash out and commit heinous mass murders. What I want this book to be is a story about what it was like to have been bullied in school, still try to live a normal life, and the effects it has on somebody as an adult.

Kids killing other kids, themselves, or just being a nuisance to society does not seem to bother people anymore. This book is about the internal torture that is created and that the person living with it could be sitting right next to you. I also touch on the bully's side, why they might be doing it, but it is NOT a free pass! I go into what may have happened to them or is happening to them. I also go into what you can do to break the cycle, on both sides.

Maybe we can spread the word a little more, open that internal struggle, and relive the experiences of what these people (bullies and bullied) went or are going through and why they decide to just end the torture or cause more torture themselves. I still suffer a great deal to this day and will go into that later, but if you know me, I do not show it. Many of the stories I am going to tell you nobody in my family has ever heard or knows about, including my wife and my mother. If they did know of some of these, they probably haven't thought about them in years. Though, I would be willing to bet, my mother knew something was going on, just not all the details. This is my story, be it what it may.

My name is Darren Sheriff, I was born on April 25th, 1966. My mother and father had not been married very long when I came along. Of course, being a baby, I do not have any recollection of what life was like in the early stages. As far as I know, things were fine. Then, on October 2nd, 1973 everything changed. I was seven years old, in second grade, and I became the man of the house. I was the oldest of three kids, the other two were my four-year-old brother and my two-year-old sister. My father passed away due to complications from diabetes.

How my mother managed everything alone still amazes me to this day. She did the impossible! They say that what you never see or didn't know about, you don't know you were supposed to have it. As far as I am concerned, I had an amazing childhood. Financially, things HAD to be tough, but I never would have guessed. We wore homemade Halloween costumes, which the kids made fun of at times, but we liked them. I especially liked the year I went as a Television, antennas and all. The Micky Mouse Club, (the cover from a coloring book) was what was on. We had what my mother called help yourself salads for dinner occasionally, it was some lunch meat, some lettuce leaves covered with oil and vinegar on a plate, I LOVED that meal! She also made a lot of soup, in huge quantities and froze it for later, and probably could write a book, the 101 uses for hamburger. To this day I can't eat Hamburger Helper, but it was all she could do at that time. I tell you all of this to lay down some foundation of where I came from. Other than my grandfather, who I saw on weekends, I had no father figure. Like I said, my mother did an amazing job, three kids, working, cooking, etc., but she could not teach me to be a man. Baseball, defending myself, working on cars, all those man type things, she was not able to teach me from a man's point of view. She did teach me some of that, plus an amazing number of other things that, in some regards, from a bullying standpoint got me in trouble. I will discuss more of that later.

My story may bring you to tears at times, you will feel hatred towards some of the people that I will talk about that did things to me. I will not give you full names, mainly because I either cannot remember what they were, or, I do not want to cause any grief to them now, they may very well be upstanding good citizens. The story I am going to tell you is 100% the truth, as well as I can recollect it. I will not be adding any fancy exaggerations, most of the time it is not needed. Some of this, many of you will blow off and say, it was just kids being kids. What you need to understand is, kids being kids, every day, builds up and will mess with your mind. Seemingly minor incidents make you feel useless, scared, and sad. Again, mine may not have been any worse that what the kids are dealing out today, I get that. Back when all of this was going on in my life, teachers were not aware of bullying, or if they were they chose to ignore it, even today many will turn a blind eye. Sometimes, they were part of the problem, not meaning to be, but added fuel to the fire. Asking for help seems easy for people to say, believe me when I say, IT IS NOT! Most of the time if you did tell a teacher about being picked on you were either told to just ignore it, suck it up, or if something was done, the abuse got worse afterward. I wish somebody had written something like what I am about to tell you then, it may have lessened some of the issues I deal with today.

After you are done reading this, I invite you to share it with your kids, they might be on one side of the bullying problem or the other, and this will get them to think.

Chapter 2-The Elementary School Years

Like I mentioned in the introduction, the early years are basically a blur. I vaguely remember going in and telling my 2nd grade teacher that my father had died, I remember her being upset. I guess I was just too young or immature to really fathom the extent of what I was telling her. I went back to playing with my classmates.

After a while, and I look back at it now, I am not completely sure when it happened, but I became very lazy. It could have been just a child's laziness, or did it have something to do with my father's passing, I have no idea. I didn't do my homework, just daydreamed during class, and did a lot of scribbling. I was not a class disrupter, I was the complete opposite, very quiet, if you closed your eyes, you did not even know I was there. I could not answer the teacher if she asked me a question, I was not paying attention. Sometimes the kids would laugh because I was fumbling around, the teacher would get upset, then move on to another student.

Third grade was kind of a joke. The teacher was very old, and I feel that all we did was arts and crafts type stuff. I remember learning how to make pom-poms in class, I think I still remember how to this day. To be honest, I could not tell you a thing else I learned in that grade.

Fourth grade, things started to escalate. I was told that I needed to start going to a speech therapist. I apparently had trouble saying things like the silly snake ate a snack. The "S" was more of a "TH". Can you imagine the ridicule that was starting to build? Again, I was probably too young or immature to be really bothered by it, but the foundation was being laid.

Then came fifth grade. I decided I wanted to start playing trombone. There was not much backlash during the initial starting of playing in the band, that was coming later, trust me. I was still in the lazy phase, I hated to practice, but it got me out of class occasionally for individual lessons. Homework and class work were usually skipped. The teacher would call me out as the laziest student she had and for all intents in purposes, gave up on me. My mother was a class helper and came in to do some class activities at times. I jumped at the chance to work with her, no school work then.

Sixth grade was another year that, to be honest, I do not remember.

That covers the elementary school years. This was in New Jersey, Middletown Village Elementary School. We lived in an old farmhouse that was easily 100 years old and out in the middle of nowhere. That is brought up because the only kids I really got to play with were my siblings. Yes, I did play during recess, but I was always a little on the chubby side, not athletic, and was always chosen last for any sports teams. So, to say I was still kind of awkward is probably an understatement.

Chapter 3-Jr. High

Here in Charleston, SC where I am living now, they call it middle school, in New Jersey, it was Junior High. Grades 7 and 8 were the only two grades at Thompson Junior High. To say I was a fish out of water does not even begin to explain the issues I was experiencing.

Band was a class, but also considered an after-school activity on occasion, so I rode the late bus home. The late bus was more for the detention students, and other unruly kids. Now, imagine a naive thirteen-year-old kid riding home with kids that are smoking, cussing, and taunting everybody and anybody that we passed on the road. The worst one was Louis. That kid scared me. He always had a knife, a cigarette, and nothing but a foul mouth. He would call me, and other shy intimidated kids, names. He would spit in our hair, mess with our hair, put ashes in the hood of our jacket, wedgies, and all the other things that you have heard about people doing to bully other kids. After school band practice was luckily only one or two days a week, I had also gotten into the Chess club, again, was an after-school activity, so I was on that late bus more days than not. My mother was working her butt off, so she could not come get me. I did walk home a couple of times, but it was miles from the school, and it seemed like it took hours.

In hindsight, I guess I was starting to really feel useless. The constant picking, pushing, spitting, etc. was starting to extract its toll. Going to the teachers was out of the question, like I mentioned earlier, unless they saw a student picking on another, it was just ignored. The bus driver basically had no authority and was laughed at. I started to hate going to school, homework, tests, etc. I was a straight D student.

I probably brought some of this on myself, being a band geek was now starting to rear its ugly head. Back in those days they taught things like metal shop, wood shop, home economics, music, and other basic classes to both boys and girls. I enjoyed the home economics course, cooking, baking, and learning some useful things. I enjoyed so much that, when it came time for me to take basic music courses, I asked to be a student assistant for the Home Eco. class. I was a band member, so basic music was something I already knew, the principal approved me being a student assistant. The name calling really began, wussy, (cleaned up to a PG-14 level), fagot, queer, wimp, and many more. This was the 70's and being called those things was common and extremely painful, especially as a child. PC was not even a thing then.

Added to the top of all of this, my clothes. My mother, bless her heart, was doing all she could, I lay no fault on her. I was not the cool kid in school with the uppity clothing, hot new sneakers, etc. We shopped at Sears which was the big store of the time. They were the only store that had the Husky Sized pants and shirts that I wore, like I said previously I was a chubby one. We did not have a lot of money as you can imagine. She had to go out and buy new school clothes every year, for three kids who, I am sure, were outgrowing things as we were trying them on. School dances came around and my mother would chaperon occasionally so I could go. I had no girlfriend, I was klutzy, overweight, and did not have on the latest fad in clothing. I felt so out of place after the first couple of dances, I never really wanted to go again. One year, before school started, we went clothes shopping, this was when the movie "Grease" first came out, and I saw a shirt with a picture of John Travolta on it, he was cool, and I desperately wanted to be. I talked my mother into buying it, big mistake. I think I wore it once to school, I was labeled gay for wearing John Travolta instead of Olivia Newton-John. I was supposed to wear the girl, not the guy. Wow have times changed.

There was also the horrible story of gym class. This class really should be outlawed. I was overweight, not athletic, hated playing any sports, and to be changing in a locker room full of a bunch of egotistical self-righteous kids is the stuff that nightmares are made of. This may be a story of kids being kids, but it is still not right. They would hide your clothes after you changed, throw things up on the rafters so you could not get them, and numerous other things. The absolute worst thing that was done to me was one of my sneakers was stolen. Sounds relatively benign, right? Well, one of my other classmates saw not only who stole it but told me where it was. It was stuffed into one of the toilets. As I was starting to fish it out, the boy who stole it walked by and stated that he also peed on it. Class was starting, and I had no choice, I pulled it out, put it on, and squished all through class. The whole time wondering if he really peed on it or not. I wanted to cry. The "coach" gym teacher just laughed and basically said, get over it.

I survived Junior High, next up was High School. I had been asked to march in the Middletown High School North Marching Band, even though I was in Junior High, and thought that if this was high school, things would be okay. The band people were fun, they were impressed that a Jr. High kid could keep up. Maybe things were going to get better, then, another major change in the family, we moved.

Chapter 4-A New Beginning?

Yes, we moved.

Not out of state, not even across the state, we moved about 7 miles, to Keansburg, NJ.

New high school, new friends, new band. Could this be a new beginning?

Apparently, kids will be kids, no matter where you live. The band was not very big. I was marching with somewhere close to 100 people in Middletown North, Keansburg had 20. We still did parades, and other concerts, plays, etc. Some of the things that happened here were no different. Even a couple of the kids in the band were jerks. Two of them were trumpet players. We were getting ready for a football game and one of them had left his uniform at home. He came to me and said that I was about his size, give me your uniform. He said he was more important on the field and that what he looked like mattered more than what I did as he was handing me a uniform 2 sizes too small. I didn't know what to do, so I took mine off and gave it to him. To make matters worse, I had on a pair of homemade suspenders made from burlap straps, they mocked me and the suspenders. I did the show but felt like I was being laughed at and stared at by the entire stadium because my uniform was way too small.

I will admit, I was not that great of a trombone player, like I said, I hated to practice. The Keansburg band seemed to be getting smaller, whether it really was or not, I am not sure. Well, the high school drama club wanted to put on a play, "Bye, Bye, Birdie" and they wanted to have a live pit orchestra. I made it into the orchestra by default, I was the only trombone player at the school. I was somewhat honored but knew deep down that I was only there because I was the only one. Well, rehearsals started, the music was tough, at least for me. The rest of the group seemed to be getting pretty good, but not me. Long story short here, the plays music director ended up cutting my part from at least half of the play. I saw the word Tacit so many times that I felt useless. There was no way in the world I could become good enough to play those parts, so I just went along. It was fun, but it was also a real blow to any ego I had.

One Memorial Day, or it might have been the Fourth of July, our cousins came over for our bi-annual BBQ picnic and cookout. We alternated the holidays that I mentioned, Memorial Day at one house, 4th of July at the other. My cousin, my brother and I were walking around town and we went down the old railroad right away past an old concrete plant or stone yard, I was never sure what it was. They had these huge mounds of stones and rocks on the other side of the fence. As we were walking by we noticed that some of the rocks had come out over to the wrong side of the fence, so we started throwing them back, thinking we were helping. Here is where hindsight comes in to play again, this was NOT a good idea, the owner/foreman whatever he was saw us throwing rocks and instead of yelling to or at us, he sent this teenage boy after us. Being that I was the oldest, he started punching, hitting, and pushing me. My cousin and brother ran off, I don’t blame them, if I could have run I would have too. Instead he landed punch after punch, blackened an eye, caused my ear to bleed, and gave me some horrific bruises. I remember all the adults suddenly showing up and them yelling at the boy. I vaguely remember walking back to the house and getting an ice pack put on my eye. I never wanted to go anywhere near that dirt right away again. I was scared, hurt, and embarrassed beyond believe. I remember one day going to the bank for somebody and the clerk asked me what happened, I told her I had gotten into a fight, she asked if the other kid looked worse, I was too embarrassed to say I never threw a punch.

Then there was the time that after a football game I was walking home, we only lived a mile or so from this school, with one of the other band members. We both had on our uniforms and carrying our horns. A car drove by and threw bottles at us, luckily, they hit us low on our bodies and not our heads. The people in the car laughed, shouted obscenities, flipped us the finger, and sped off. My buddy said that he was glad to be getting out of there soon, his family was moving, he was tired of seeing people like us being picked on.

This high school also taught things like metal and wood shop, I hated both. I had no artistic talent for these kinds of things. Once, in metal shop, the project was to cut out and make a sconce. Hammer the metal out, solder some brass for the candle to be placed in, and create a hook for the back for it to hang. There were more kids in the class than there was equipment to be used, so I always got pushed aside by the bigger, bolder students, so they could use that equipment. When the final days of that project came around, the teacher held up everybody's finished product for the class to see, mine was way below standard, and was mocked. I even remember the teacher saying something along the lines of how this one should fail, he did not know it was mine, but it was.

That metal shop classroom holds other very bad memories. It just so happens that we had a Homeroom class every day for announcements, the Pledge of Allegiance, etc., mine was in the metal shop classroom. There was a punk in my homeroom, I don't even remember his name, but he had long dirty blond hair, wore AC/DC shirts, smoked, and looking back was probably high half the time, his eyes always seemed bloodshot. He picked on me mercilessly, he is the reason I believe that I have no children. I cannot prove it, but the wife and I had tried for many years. He would walk up to me and literally just knock me in the groin. My apologies to all the guys reading this, I know you just grimaced. This was back in the early 80's, in 2010 there was a fad being talked about called, "sack tapping" or "ball tapping," as it is called, a boy will try to slap or flick the groin of another boy to inflict discomfort or pain. I guess I was the test pattern for a new fad way before it was a fad.

I tried to stay away from this kid and the pain he inflicted, but it was useless in the small classroom. I tried to talk to the teacher, but I think he was afraid of this punk as much as I was. There was no way I could tell my mother, how embarrassing is that conversation going to be, "Mom, there is a kid hitting me in the nuts.

I was only at Keansburg High for just shy of two years. In the latter part of my Sophomore year, it was announced we would be moving again. This time it would be out of state, we are heading south, Florida is our destination. Clearwater to be exact.

Chapter 5-The Florida Years

Clearwater Florida was a place that was, to some extent, familiar. We had vacationed there a few times, and it was a very pretty city. So, maybe, oh please, maybe, this will be the start of something good.

In all honesty, the Florida years were not bad. Yes, I came in during the middle of a semester, but the transition was not horrible. Apparently, I was a little bit ahead of the Florida school system, so even though I never studied, I was at least now a C student.

The first full year of band was tough, Mr. Hacker was the band director. He was known to throw chairs during rehearsals, but overall, he was loved. He died that January of my junior year. He was replaced by Robert W. Smith. This man was an angel in disguise! He is listed as my number one most awesome teacher of all time! He saw things in me, taught me so much, and I will never forget him. I truly wish I could have been his student for a much longer time. I still never really did fit in at school, except with the band geeks (affectionately called that now) the band was honorable in Clearwater. We won state championships and were just an all-round great entity.

Even though it was not considered bad times, Florida did have some pitfalls. I started my first job at Burger King. Again, I may have been 17 physically, but, I would imagine that mentally I was much younger. I did not know what was expected of me, the girl that was training me was short tempered and abrupt. If I messed up, she jumped on me. So, when it was slow, I knew sweeping was good to do. Apparently not. She told me that I would never be able to keep a job if all I did was sweep and that I needed to get some brains and learn how to work here. Again, I was crushed. However, as a side note, I did eventually learn the job and then some, when I left there, I was the training person. I was now teaching the new people what to do, but, I was ALWAYS second guessing myself. I was worried that I was doing it wrong, or that the newbie would do something that was not how I showed them but would report it as I did. I was good, on the outside, but inside, I had zero confidence.

A few other things that shook my confidence were, I failed my written driving test which is normal for many teens, but remember, I was already on shaky ground in the confidence field. Girlfriends were numerous, but again, that is a teens nightmare already. The night of graduation was a little scary. I was dressed up in my cap and gown, ready to walk the stage, and I was not even sure they were going to let me graduate. A message had come to me stating that I was short one P.E. class and that it had to be made up or no graduation. Was it a joke or was it for real? To this day, I am not completely sure, I did receive my diploma, but the entire couple of hours I was a nervous wreck.

Something that, I can't say was a confidence issue on my part, but something that really rattled my world was what happened when we first moved to Florida. It was a military move and a box of some of my most precious items were lost. Things that my grandfather had given me, vinyl records, trombone mutes, and many other items. Like I said, not a confidence crusher, but just another thorn in the side to make you feel vulnerable and useless. Why would somebody steal those things from me?

Living in Florida came to abrupt end not too very long after I graduated in 1984. My stepfather was being transferred again, this time to Charleston, South Carolina.

Chapter 6-Moving On

Charleston, SC, and we were in one of the suburbs, Summerville to be more specific. It was a nice quite neighborhood, I was out of school now and had the world in front of me. I worked a few places, again at Burger King, and then I went into the convenience store business working the graveyard shift. I was still an uneasy, no confidence person, but I was getting good at hiding it by now. If you were to walk up to me you would think I was stable, but I was cowering underneath.

I am a very astute watcher. I would watch people all the time and try to mimic what they did. If they seemed to have it all together, then maybe that is what I should do. I put it to the test one night. One of the responsibilities of the graveyard shift was to stock the cooler of soda, beer, juice, etc. I was trying my best to do a good job and do it to the best of my ability. Put the correct items in the correct places. Well, somebody on the day shift had screwed that all up, there were labels after all, why can't you put things in the proper place? I was tired of pulling all the wrong stock out and replacing it with the correct items, or, if there wasn't any, leave it empty, as per the store managers request. I left a note one night in the cooler explaining all of this and that I was getting tired of fixing it. Hell has no wrath than a coworker that has been outed. I had the entire staff come down on me, I tried to explain that I was just doing my job. The crux of the problem? I should not have left the note but instead go to the person and explain it to them. That is not possible if you don't know who it is. The note was not mean, not pointed at anybody directly, just explaining the situation.

The takeaway I want you to get from this is, try to see what it is like from the other person's point of view. I felt that I was the idiot and that no matter how hard I try, I cannot and will not ever measure up.

Moving on, I decided I might want to get back into music, so I applied to Baptist College, now Charleston Southern University. I was accepted and started a career path towards a music education degree. The trombone part wasn't bad, I finally had gotten at least bearable to listen to playing. The theory, dictation, and piano lessons were another whole story. I failed my first semester of music theory and was about to get kicked out of the school when suddenly, the theory teacher died. I buffaloed my way back into the class with his replacement, he was much easier to learn from. I never did well in any of the college classes, even the music ones, I doubted myself too much and could never really put it together.

Confidence and I were nowhere even close to being on speaking terms. One day, I had a crazy idea of auditioning for the U.S. Navy Band. I got the audition setup, practiced, and thought I would be a shoe in.

Fail.

He said that there were no openings for trombones right now, but you could join up and go into Nuclear Submarines and then eventually transfer over. From what I was told, that would NEVER happen, once Nuclear, always Nuclear. Well, the navy cat that auditioned me was a friend of my mothers and had a friend that was an Army recruiter, He asked if I would like to audition for the Army, I can give him a call. Navy was my first choice, but I figured sure, why not.

A couple of days later, I get a call from the Army recruiter. We talked a while and he told me that we can do an audition but there are no openings for a trombonist in any of the field bands. Would you like to join up as something else and then eventually transfer over? I politely told him no, I really want to be a musician. I thought that was the end of that. Now what? I was probably putting more pressure on myself than anything, but I was already feeling like a total failure now and I needed to do something with my life.

I believe it was the next day that a Marine Corps recruiter called me and told me he had been in conversation with the Army recruiter and wanted to know if I would like to audition for the U.S. Marine Corps. I was stunned, but thought, sure, what have I got to lose. We set the audition up for a few weeks away, he would drive me down to Parris Island to play in front of some of the nation's best military musicians.

I passed.

Little did I know that was the start to a whole new world of confidence deterioration and rebuilding.

Boot Camp was the hardest thing I think I have ever done. The mission of Boot Camp is to tear you down to nothing, then rebuild you into a lean mean fighting machine. The tear down was pretty much a given, I did that for them the first 22 years or so of my life. The rebuilding part almost did not work. I barely graduated Boot Camp, the physical requirements were almost too much for chubby old me. I could shoot a weapon and had the knowledge to kill people, but I never really had a lot of confidence in myself. Granted, I had more than I ever had before in my life, but it was not anywhere close to what it should have been. I am eternally grateful for my time in the Corps, I will always be a U.S. Marine, but I never really felt like I made a good one. Never really measured up in my own eyes. I was disciplined for my lack of physical abilities more times than I care to remember and even my playing abilities were lacking in comparison, though I was much better of a player than I had ever been in college. I was extended at the School of Music twice for failing to make the passing grade, they give you 30 days extension to improve your playing or drop out/get kicked out. I did finally graduate, but it was by the slimmest of margins.

I spent the year after the school of music in Okinawa, Japan. My fiancé and I had to postpone our wedding for that year. Long distance relationships are hard, being 13 hours in time difference is even harder. The stress was tough, but we made it and in January of 1992, I came home and was married.

I look back over my four-year career in the Corps and I am glad I did it. On the eve of me leaving I sat on the back steps with a Gunnery Sergeant who was very wise, and he tried to give me some good advice. You are leaving the

Corps, be proud of what you have accomplished, and look forward to the possibilities of a new beginning. He knew that I was lacking in self-confidence, I am not sure how, or if anybody else did, but he did.

After the Corps, life was up and down.

Trying To Put It All Behind Me

Chapter 7-Starting the Married Life

When I got out of the Marine Corps, it was January 1994. I was married to the love of my life and had no idea of where I was going next. When I got out, we were living in Jacksonville, North Carolina and we hated that place. So anywhere else would be good. I figured I would put my G.I. Bill to good use, go back to school and become that band teacher I started out to be years ago. So, I applied to different colleges and Northwestern State University of Louisiana accepted me. They were in Natchitoches, Louisiana so onward the wife and I headed.

There are many things in life that look good on paper, this was one of them. Newly married, no money, you must find a job to eat, live somewhere, etc. I have heard of people being able to pull this off, I guess I was just not strong enough. I ended up selling Kirby vacuum cleaners for 3 or 4 months. If you have never done that kind of work, I highly DO NOT recommend it! Basically, you go into a person's house, carrying a vacuum that costs $1200 and try to convince them it is the greatest thing since sliced bread. I did this in hopes of getting enough money to get going in school. No such luck. After that failure, I went and applied as a cashier at a convenience store/gas station. I had gotten enrolled in school and was ready to start classes. Well, reality was starting to weigh down on me. Trying to go to school during the day, work at a convenience store at night, I knew I wasn't going to be able to pull that off. Who was I fooling, there was no way I had the confidence to even try. So, school fell by the wayside. I kept telling myself, I will go back someday.

Someday.

The convenience store life was interesting. I ended up being the second half of the "A Team" as the store manager called us. Susan Williams was the other half. She ended up being a great friend to both me and the wife. We keep in touch even to this day. The store was only about 2 miles from the trailer we were living in. We had a car for a short time, but the engine blew up. I literally pieced together a bicycle from parts that I found in people's trash. That wasn't so bad, I liked bike riding and besides, I was a Marine and the exercise was good for me.

Well, there were some "regulars" that hung around that store that were not of the highest caliper shall we say. Drunks, thieves, and hoodlums are more like it. They would do all kinds of things to my poor bicycle for spite. Hiding it in the dumpster, taking it for joy rides, and just mocking me around it while I tried to work. I remember one night that they literally stepped on the wheels and bent them so bad that they would not turn. I straightened them up enough that I could at least push it home that night and worked on it the next day to get it functional again. The police could not/would not do anything about it because in their words, "they are just goofing around". Yes, they would talk to them and it would stop for a couple of days, but then it would start back up, even more aggressively. Visions of high school were rearing their ugly head. Could I have just gone out and beat the crap out of them? Maybe, but they were many and I was one. So, I just kept on plugging away at my job doing the best I could. The district manager took a liking to me and my work ethic, so, I ended up managing my own store. I was the manager for a little over a year. I still biked to work, roughly 3 or 4 miles, but it was still not bad. After my store got robbed twice, it was time to get out of that place. The district manager teared up my last day there, he really thought I was doing a good job, but I just did not feel safe anymore. My mother worked for a company that was looking for store managers in Maine. More money, closer to my family, and NOT in Louisiana. North bound, bound we were.

Maine was a very short visit for a couple of reasons. Even though I am originally from New Jersey, I do not like the cold anymore. If you have never been to Maine, there is a LOT of cold up there. Then, come to find out, there was a bunch of theft going on in my store. You know the theory, no matter what, the head honcho takes the blame, so I was canned. The wife was working at a type of big box store of the time, Ames Department store, as a cashier, I ended up getting a job as a stocker. Even between the two of us, the ends never met. It is extremely expensive to live up there. As we were sitting in the living room one night, I made the statement along the lines of, this is stupid, we can't make ends meet, we are living like paupers, we need to do something. I then suggested we go back to Charleston, South Carolina, Tammy's home town, a place where I have lots of contacts, friends, and Tammy's family who she missed badly.

As you can imagine, this was kind of a hard pill to swallow. I couldn't go back to school, was a manager of a couple of different convenience stores that had many issues, some of my own doing, some not, but they were on my watch. I was still being picked on, made fun of, and I could not make enough money to support my family and live a halfway decent life. I kept running away, or so it felt, trying to see if I could ever amount to anything. So, back to Charleston to see what we could do there.

Chapter 8-Back in Charleston

We came back to Charleston in August of 1997. Tammy started working at Marshall's Department store and as of September 2018 she is still there. I, on the other hand, tried an array of different jobs. First as an assistant manager at a Hess Gas station. It was bringing back a lot of bad memories and jumped at the chance when I saw an ad for a vending route operator of a potato chip company. This job wasn't the most horrible thing I have ever done. Basically, I drove around town restocking vending machines in department stores, schools, and other business'. The money wasn't great, but, if you worked hard, you could do okay. I did just that, I busted my butt! I asked questions at all my stops to see what they really wanted, pulled things out that didn't sell and replaced them with stuff that did. My route was really starting to come together. Then, the route manager, his name was Ernie, looked at my route doing well and one of the other guys route that wasn't. He decided to take some of my good ones and give them to the other guy and wanted me to build up some of his bad ones. I really did NOT think it was fair, but after some deep thinking I took it on as a challenge to see what I could do. So, the building began. It was going well, I was starting to build some confidence. A couple of months later, he did it again! After that, I figured that apparently, I just couldn't do anything else for this company and left. I moved on to a different company, basically doing the same thing. I was not thrilled by how this company did things and left them after only a couple of months. Having to pay for your own vehicle maintenance was ludicrous, they didn't pay that much to begin with.

The one thing those two companies did for me at least was give me experience at driving larger trucks. There was an ad in the paper for a truck driver at a local wholesale florist company. I applied and got that job. Again, this was not a horrible job. I drove a great big refrigerated truck full of cut flowers to different florists and sold them. I was in Myrtle Beach twice a week, Savannah, Ga twice a week and the remaining day I had the boonies run as I called it, through many small towns up through the heart of South Carolina. I learned so much about flowers doing this and it would come in handy later. I was there for about 2 years. The owner ended up firing his partner and things started to go south financially. I left before it went totally belly up, which it has since then. Before I left though, I had applied for a job that would basically send my life into a whole new, exciting future, except for one major hiccup which I will get to in a little bit.

The new job was still driving a delivery truck, it was a 30-foot horse trailer, and the delivery product was plants and trees. The company name was Lowcountry Nursery, the owner Ron Kabool (Who was one of the people I dedicated my second book to, "A Beginner's Guide to Lowcountry Gardening & Landscaping") was one of, if not the greatest bosses I will ever have. Ron was stern, but fair, if you screwed up he let you know it, then five minutes later acted as if it never happened. He was always open to answering any questions I had about plants, the industry, etc. He knew

I had a passion for horticulture before I even did. My immediate supervisor, Bob McKenzie (the other person I dedicated book number two too) was like a father to me. He also must have seen my passion and desire to learn the trade. Between the two of them they encouraged me to learn, paying for many of the classes that I took, including becoming a Master Gardener and a Certified Professional Nurseryman. They took/sent me to trade shows, introduced me to all the right people, and were very instrumental in me becoming The Citrus Guy as so many in the trade knows me as. I figured I was going to retire from Lowcountry Nursery, or at least stay there until something big came along. I was there for 12 years, until……

March 30th, 2014 the beginning of the end happened. Ron passed away from cancer. It was his second bout of it. A year or so before his passing, he had developed esophageal cancer. They went in, removed it, and Ron seemed to be getting better. Then, he took a turn for the worse. He started to feel bad again, was losing weight like crazy, and just looked weak and frail. The doctors decided to open him up again and see what was going on. The exploratory surgery did not last long at all. The doctor opened him up, looked inside and said, close him back up, there is nothing we can do. The cancer had returned, it had returned with a vengeance, and was everywhere. The day that he passed away will forever be etched in my memory. They say that when major events happen you can remember exactly where you were and what you were doing, use the example of 9/11 if you were born then. I will bet you know exactly what you were doing, where you were, and how you first heard about that. In my case, and Ron's death, it was a Sunday and I was sitting in my recliner chair watching a NASCAR race when I received the phone call. The emotions I experienced were overwhelming. We knew he was bad, but if you knew Ron, you knew for sure he would beat this thing. It didn't happen.

Monday came, and we broke the news to all the rest of the employees, all the while trying to figure out what to do. The nursery would remain open until after the reading of the will and we would go from there. Bob was now in charge. We attempted to keep things as normal as possible, but as you can imagine, it wasn't easy. There were other players in this game that I will not mention their names, since, well it wasn't pretty, and I REALLY dislike most of them to this day. Due to some backstabbing and just plain old evilness, Bob was accused of some stuff and he decided to quit, later I found out it was all fabricated against him, hence my dislike for some of the other players. Well, Bob's last day was on Friday, April 25th, 2014, my birthday. I was approached and asked if I could run the nursery until the apparent sale was finalized. I wanted to stay employed, there were 15 other people that needed to keep working, and if I wouldn't/couldn't the nursery would shut down right then and there. What was I going to say? So, out of nowhere I hear myself saying, "absolutely". In a way I was honored. The place that I loved, that had helped me to learn so much, that I thought I was going to work at forever, was now under my command! I was also petrified!!

The following Monday, when I officially took over, everybody shows up to work as usual and we have a meeting telling everybody the situation. It was not met with open arms by everybody, but we were going to make it work. There was a lot of blood, sweat, and tears, mostly mine! The lawyer had told me to, "just maintain the current status, do not try to grow the company". I really had NO IDEA what she meant, but I would just take it a day at a time. There were a LOT of shenanigans being played by the people you were really in control. They wanted me to run the nursery, but had my hands tied at every turn. Even with all the restrictions in place, and not even really trying, our sales kept going up. The sale of the nursery seemed to be dragging on and on and on. Purposely? I may never know. By the April of 2015 we were having almost record sales, with practically no staff. Everybody was reading the writing on the wall and looking for other employment, I could not blame them. Those of us that were still there were taking on more and more responsibilities. I even tried to quit once, but I basically was told that I couldn't and just hang on a little longer. Tension and frustration were taking its toll. We were all physically, mentally, and emotionally exhausted. I was not only in charge, but I had resumed my role as delivery driver, I was the only one that could drive the truck!

Then, it happened......

The Day the World Stopped

Chapter 9-The World Stopped

Let me give you a quick recap.

I had been bullied a good bit of my life and had no self-esteem or confidence. I was always afraid of making decisions because I had no confidence in myself. I was always told that what I did was wrong, or that I was lazy, or would not amount to anything. I literally went from truck/delivery driver to managing a multi-million-dollar nursery in the blink of an eye. Making all kinds of huge decisions, financially, personnel, and logistically. Plus, I had my hands tied by the real decision makers, who were making all kinds of bad choices, and who knows what other "deals" behind the scenes. It was crazy!

May 11th, 2015- The day my world stopped.

It was a Monday. I went in to the nursery early as usual to open. As I stood there at my desk, a sudden wave of depression, worse that I had ever had before, came over me. It had been slowly getting worse and worse as the days dragged on. Christmas the previous December sucked, because I was burned out, tired, and depressed. As the new year went on, I thought more and more about how to end this. The nursery had to go on, there were others that depended on it, like I said earlier, I tried to quit, but couldn't. How else could I end this? By ending me.

The thought had crossed my mind many times. Depression and I were very intimate with each other. I came up with all kinds of ways to end it. A gun, overdose, jump in front of a truck, the list went on and on. Each time the waves of depression hit me, it felt like a house had fallen on me. Sleeping at night, or at least trying to, was miserable. The dreams and the sudden claustrophobic/panic attacks in the middle of the night made everything even worse. I kept telling myself that it will be better soon, this will all be over, and the nursery will get sold, life will go on. It worked for a while.

That day that my world stopped, I could not take it anymore. As soon as the first person came in, I told them I had to run an errand and I will be back soon. They looked at me odd but said okay. They knew I was upset but did not ask. My errand? I had one last choice, go seek help, or end this hell I was living, As you have probably figured by now, I did the first one. I drove down to the VA Hospital, went right up to the information desk and asked the poor guy there, "I need to talk to somebody before I kill myself!". I was in tears by now, and the look on his face suggested that I scared the crap out of him. He sent me to the fifth floor where I repeated that same sentence to the woman working that desk. She asked me a couple of questions, told me that everything was going to be alright, and that I did a very brave thing by coming to the hospital. She had me sit down, very close so she could keep an eye on me and said somebody will be out in a minute.

To be honest, I only have a few vague memories, pieces more precisely, of what happened that first hour or two after my initial contact with the hospital. I know I talked to a couple of doctors, both male and female, names I have no idea. I know one had me call my wife and I remember telling her over and over again how sorry I was as I cried uncontrollably. I know they asked if I would mind staying there at the hospital for a few days for observation, I agreed. They took me down to the third floor, 3A to be exact, the mental health ward. After getting checked in, given my robe, and being shown my room, I laid on my bed for hours, crying and thinking to myself, what have I done!

I spent three and half days on 3A, sleeping a good part of it. I was exhausted and worn out. When I was awake, if there was not some kind of volunteer talking to the group, I stared out the window and thought, deep thoughts. There was limited phone access, so I could not talk much to anybody outside the hospital, I did talk to my wife a couple of times, but that was the extent of outside communications. No phone, no computer, not even my watch. After the first two days I really started feeling better. I had gotten some good rest and did some deep thinking. I knew things must have felt like they were looking up because I started being concerned about my plants at home and would ask any of the nurses when they came in if they knew if it had rained in North Charleston. They had mountains of reading material, nothing I would read. Mostly novels, romance, a few history books, etc. I asked the nursing staff onetime if they knew of any botany books or upper level horticultural books that might have been on the hospital premises somewhere. They made a few phone calls, but there was nothing.

The third day, one of the psychiatrists came in to talk to me and said that I had been asking for some strange books. I told her the story, that had been told to others for what seemed like the thousandth time, and she commented that I seemed in good spirits, which by then, I was. I asked her if I could leave, she said, tell you what, you are still in this kind of mood tomorrow, we will make it happen. And I was, and they did!

I went home that Thursday after lunch. By then, Lowcountry Nursery had cut me loose, came and stole back their company vehicle, even though I told them I was going to bring it to them Friday. I did feel a LOT better, my dog and wife were very happy I was home, but now I was jobless and shaken to the core, confidence level now at negative 15%.

I tell you all of this, not to illicit sympathy, but to give you the idea of how far to the bottom I had gone, and where we are going next.

Chapter 10-Putting it Together

So, here we are, at the bottom of the well.

THIS, is where I really want you to start paying attention if you haven't been. I will encompass a lot of conclusions, thoughts, and pieces of things for YOU to be thinking about.

I dodged a bullet (mild pun intended)

I did a lot of thinking about my past, where I was at this time, and the future. I am not going to go all religious on you, but, apparently, I have/had a reason for not just ending it all. Hopefully, this book is one of those things and I help somebody.

I have a full-time job, literally minutes away from the house that I can say I enjoy again. I have two books that I have authored with many more in the pipeline already. My lecture schedule is abundant, I am ready for Camellia season to begin for the friendly competition and camaraderie of those people. I am more confident, at times, of what I am doing. Not a day goes by that I do not help somebody with garden, horticultural, or citrus question. I pick up my trombone occasionally and have fun with my brass group, especially around Christmas time. My wife and puppies are always eager to see me come home. I am glad I did not end it all.

Suicide is NOT the easy way out! It may be for the individual but stop and think about your family. It is a very selfish thing to do, especially if nobody knows why. PLEASE, do not get me wrong, I understand the whole situation is a Catch 22, you are depressed because you have been bullied, your life is not going the way you wanted it to, you feel lost, hopeless, and useless. I have heard many people say things like, why didn't they just ask for help? They can't. To ask for help just deepens the feelings of guilt, uselessness, and despair. It is a horrible circle of events, asking for help makes you feel weak, then the thoughts of, if you weren't so weak and useless, you wouldn't feel like this. Why can't somebody help me, oh yeah, I am too useless for anybody to care, so why bother.

Your loved ones, parents, siblings, grandparents, and friends will wonder what they missed, could they have helped? They can at least speak to each other, maybe try to make some sense of it. Now, think about your pet. Your dog or cat, or whatever, they won't understand why you never come home. They have nothing in their life except you. My wife and my dog are probably the two biggest things in my life and that is why I did not do the ultimate.

Can you see how being bullied can affect the world? If you are on the receiving end of it, there seems like there is no end in sight. If you are on the giving side of it, what does it really accomplish? You must belittle somebody to make yourself feel bigger and better? You come from a well to do family and have those $200 sneakers, meanwhile, there is a kid that has only one parent, barely making ends meet, and they can't afford anything better than a $10 pair of shoes. Does that make you feel good?

My life has gotten much better since the day my world stopped. Is it perfect? Not a chance. Have I helped change many people's lives, for the better? ABSOLUTELY, you better believe that! There are still many days when I feel as if I am being picked on, mocked, etc. Is it really happening? NO! It is all in my mindset. I should not take everything personally, but I do, I know that it is not usually meant that way. I have ideas on how things should go, and they get shot down. Again, I start feeling like they are personal attacks, which they are not. I must keep reminding myself of this every day.

I am sure you have probably heard of "Helicopter Parents" and possibly even the newest moniker, "Lawnmower Parents"? If not here are portions of an article, **(https://www.weareteachers.com/lawnmower-parents/)** about those lawnmower parents. Basically, lawnmower parents go to whatever lengths necessary to prevent their child from having to face adversity, struggle, or failure. Instead of preparing children for challenges, they mow obstacles down so kids won't experience them in the first place.

A child who has never had to deal with conflict on their own will not approach the first test they bomb in college and say, "Yikes. I really need to study harder. I'll reach out to the graduate assistant and see if they know of study groups I can join or other materials I can read to do better on the next one." Instead, they will very likely respond in one or more of the following ways:

Blame the professor

Call home and beg their parents to intervene
Have a mental breakdown or make themselves miserable
Write nasty reviews online about the professor and their class
Begin planning for the inevitable destruction of their college career/future
Assume they failed because they're stupid
Collapse in on themselves and give up completely and stop trying

I promise, this is not where my lack of confidence is coming from. The author and I of the article I mentioned above, have clinical anxiety that can feel crippling at times and we have struggled with often throughout our childhood. In my case, being bullied just multiplied that anxiety. But I can't even imagine how much worse it would be if my parents (just Mother in my case) had taught me that my anxiety was something to be feared and avoided, not dealt with head-on; had I been raised to shy away from anything outside of my comfort zone instead of the work and process through my discomfort; had I received the message as a child that my parents—NOT ME—were the only ones equipped to handle the challenges in my life. My story might have a completely different ending!

Do you want a clue as to if you are in the presence of a possibly bullied, depressed person? Humor. Yes, humor is a possible sign. CNN recently did an article about The Sad Clown Paradox. Robin Williams, Richard Pryor, and Ellen Degeneres all suffer from mental issues. "I despised myself from pretty much close to getting out of the womb," comedian

Richard Lewis said in a documentary. "I was always wrong. Let's start with that. When you are always wrong, you seek an audience to disprove that theory."

There was a study done where, participants (comedians) felt as if they understood themselves well and had good relationships, yet they often felt "misunderstood, picked on or bullied." They were also more likely to be "angry, suspicious and depressed" compared with those outside that profession. In the CNN documentary, comedian Patton Oswalt agrees: "A lot of comedians are people that are very introverted, very shy, very sensitive to humiliation. The only way to combat it is to go to the one place where you are stripped bare." It is theorized that humor can leave the comedian with a feeling of control over a situation in which they would otherwise be powerless. The great comedian Robin Williams is credited with saying, "I think the saddest people always try their hardest to make people happy because they know what it's like to feel absolutely worthless and they don't want anyone else to feel like that."

I can truly attest to that. I have a mantra or self-ingrained purpose, I have to make at least one person laugh, every day. Laughter is truly music to my ears.

If you're that depressed, reach out to someone. And remember, suicide is a permanent solution, to a temporary problem. That is also a Robin Williams quote, sadly, he did not take his own advice.

I DO NOT WANT THAT TO HAPPEN TO YOU!!!

Hopefully, you have a trusted friend that you can confide in? Let them know how you feel, even if only vaguely to get it started. If you don't have anybody that you feel you can trust, I have more information below.

If you're thinking about suicide, are worried about a friend or loved one, or would like emotional support, the Lifeline network is available 24/7 across the United States. **1-800-273-8255.** The Lifeline is available for everyone, it is free, and confidential.

No matter what problems you're dealing with, whether you're thinking about suicide, if you need someone to lean on for emotional support, call the Lifeline.

People call to talk about lots of things: substance abuse, economic worries, relationships, sexual identity, getting over abuse, depression, mental and physical illness, and loneliness, to name a few.

Believe it or not, even just writing things down can be helpful. Writing this book has helped me uncover many skeletons in my own closet and now maybe it will get easier. I am not saying you need to write a book, unless you want to. A diary can be an awesome thing! The only person that needs to see it is you, write down what you want to say to somebody, things you want to do, how you feel, etc. Then, when/if you think you should reach out to someone, hand them your diary. Tell them up front, this is just how I felt on certain days, it will make it easier to break the ice.

Chapter 11-The Bully's Side

Now, to the other side of the coin!

Hopefully, maybe, you are reading this book because you have been accused of bullying and somebody thought it might be a good idea for you to read this to see what kind of damage you are doing.

Good for Them!

I am NOT going to give you a free pass here. I understand that there might be reasons for why you are acting this way, it does NOT mean that it is right!

According to a recent study by **us.ditchthelabel.org**, 66% of the people who had admitted to bullying somebody else were male. Take a minute to think about how guys are raised in our culture and compare that to the ways in which girls are raised. The moment a guy starts to show any sign of emotion, he's told to man up and to stop being a girl. For girls, it's encouraged that they speak up about issues that affect them. For guys, it's discouraged and so they start to respond with aggressive behaviors, such as bullying, as a way of coping with issues that affect them. Therefore, guys are more likely than girls to physically attack somebody or to commit crimes.

You still need to understand that it is wrong, VERY WRONG to bully somebody.

There is a GREAT website that gives seven ways to stop from being a bully.

It is: **https://www.ditchthelabel.org/how-to-stop-bullying-others**
I would like to give examples of a few things from that site.

Bullying is a learned behavior and is often used as a coping mechanism for a stressful situation. Common examples could include being bullied by somebody else, abuse, a traumatic situation or a stressful home life. In addition, we also know that some people bully others because they may feel competitive towards them or may not fully understand an element about them.

What is the one thing that we all have in common? Stress. We all feel it, but it's important to recognize stress and deal with it accordingly. By that, we mean - don't store it up and let it fester, as it can have significant impacts on your mood and health. Now, put yourself in the shoes of the person you are bullying, they didn't do anything to you, so why are you stressing them?

If you get nothing else from all of this, here is the most important fact of all.

To you, it may not seem serious, but to another person, the impact could be significant. For every 10 people who are bullied, 3 of them will self-harm, 1 will go on to have a failed suicide attempt and 1 will develop an eating disorder. Additionally, we know that people who have been bullied, on average, achieve lower grades and therefore the bullying could reduce their future career prospects.
Still feel all powerful, Mr. Bully?

Chapter 12-Final Conclusions

Again, this book is NOT about me and my need to be felt sorry for. I told you all these events of mine to give you the flavor of what may or may not constitute bullying. Some of these may seem very minor, almost stupid that I mentioned them. I have come to grips with the way I look and feel, even though I still suffer many times, I love to make people laugh, I can, and will make fun of myself.

Here is a picture I put on Facebook for some fun to freak out my baby brother just before his wedding. I told him this was what I was going to wear.

The theme was Garden Casual, and I was going for both! This was NOT something I would have done 20 years ago, but I have gotten better since then.

Go ahead, Laugh. I can hear you.

Like I said, some of my stories may have seemed minor, or petty to you. With my apologies, The Dalai Lama once said, 'If you think you are too small to make a difference, try sleeping with a mosquito', translate that to 'If you think an event is too small, try being spit on every day for a thousand days'. My point is, just because it seems like nothing to you, it could be the straw that breaks the camel's back.

I would love for all bullying to stop, and all depression to come to an end, sadly, it probably won't. If your reading this and it makes one more person realize that what they are doing is wrong and detrimental to not only that person, but to society, it will have done its job.

Here and in the previous chapter I mentioned different professional groups to contact to talk to, I understand that is tough. I want to put it out there, if you just can't get yourself to talk to any of them, PLEASE, e-mail me. TheCitrusGuy@netzero.com

I have been there, I want to help, no judgments from me, I COMPLETELY understand. A friendly ear is all I want to offer.

Some other good professional contacts are:

Feeling depressed? Get free help now

Text CONNECT to 741741 in the United States.

https://www.stopbullying.gov/

Cyber Bullying: **https://www.netsmartz.org/Home**

http://www.pacer.org/bullying/

As a final parting shot, if you see somebody being bullied, and you deem it safe, please step in and stop it. If you are uncomfortable, report it, to anybody of some authority, teacher, bus driver, principle, crossing guard, school nurse, anybody that can help. Check out some of the above websites and contact somebody there.

You very well could be saving a life!!

About the Author

This book, while not anywhere NEAR what I usually write, was inspired by many recent events, too many to name. I wanted to let you know that, while this book is completely factual, it is not my usual genre. What I put myself out there now is this.

Darren Sheriff is a Certified Professional Nurseryman, a Charleston County Master Gardener and is the Manager for Terra Bella Garden Center in North Charleston, South Carolina. Darren has been in the Nursery and Garden Center industry since 2003 but has basically been a gardener all his life. He originates from New Jersey and kindly asks that you don't hold that against him, with a chuckle.

Better known as "The Citrus Guy" in the Lowcountry he has more than 55 different varieties of citrus in his yard, all in containers. Darren is the founder and current President of the Lowcountry Fruit Growers Society as well as the current President of the Coastal Carolina Camellia Society. As an accredited Camellia Flower judge, he judges and competes throughout much of the southeast. His love of Camellias goes beyond normal, having over 220 Camellias in his yard and is the South Carolina American Camellia Society State Director as well as a board member of the American Camellia Society.

He loves education and teaching, so he started a gardening blog to help extend that mission. It is not only educational but also sometimes funny and hopefully always inspirational. It can be found at **http://thecitrusguy.blogspot.com/**.

Darren has a deep passion for helping people with their problems in and out of the garden. Look him up on Facebook as The Real Citrus Guy or you can contact him at TheCitrusGuy@netzero.com for your questions about this or any of his other books, your garden, or pretty much anything relating to the horticultural world. He wants you to e-mail him if you just need a friendly ear.

His books can be found on his bookstore by following the links on his website.

His website is **http://thecitrusguy.com/**

There is also an impromptu interview and links to his books at https://www.smashwords.com/profile/view/TheCitrusGuy

www.ingramcontent.com/pod-product-compliance
Lightning Source LLC
Chambersburg PA
CBHW040236240726
48664CB00001B/150

* 9 7 8 1 7 2 7 0 3 4 4 4 8 *